Beautifully
CHANGED

Beautifully CHANGED

MISSY WAITERS

Beautifully Changed Book Publishing

Atlanta, Georgia

Beautifully CHANGED
Published by:
Beautifully Changed Book Publishing
toniawaiters.tw@gmail.com

Missy Waiters, Publisher
QualityPress.Info, Book Packager

Copyright © 2020 by Tonia Waiters
ISBN #: 978-1-0879112-8-1
Library of Congress Control Number: 2020917482

DEDICATION

Dedicated to my son Brandon. I'm so sorry for every mistake; they were never from a lack of love, but from a lack of understanding. I loved you when I first saw you. You have seen me fall and have cheered me on. For your forgiveness and love, thank you buddy. I am super proud of you.

ACKNOWLEDGEMENTS

To my mother, thank you for a love that never wavered. No matter how old I get, I will always need you. To my sister, thank you for always showing up when I needed you the most. You both are priceless in my eyes.

To my mentor, Apostle Zelda Robinson I appreciate you. For taking me under your wing and showing me the difference that a relationship with GOD can do in your life… thank you.

To my babe, I didn't realize when I met you how much of a treasure I was getting. Thank you for walking with me and being my friend.

Beautifully CHANGED

CONTENTS

PREFACE
DREAMING DOES MATTER

I am no expert. I have no degrees under my belt. My qualifications are not born out of any type of schooling except the school of hard knocks. My life experiences have gotten me from there to here, from being homeless to be a homeowner. I have gone from being desperate for the love of a man to choosing to love and be loved. I am just a girl from a small town of West Virginia with big dreams and if not now, when? And so it is that I also ask you, if not now, when? If you do not finish that book, then when? If you do not work on your marriage, then when? We can spend years saying that we will do it later or do it tomorrow, but now is all we really have.

Y'all know that saying that we hear in church, "tomorrow is not promised." We have to be intentional about changing our life. This book will give readers an opportunity to reflect upon their own life upbringing and situation, and apply the habits that I have learned. Surround yourself with positive people with whom you can grow. Bishop Jakes said, "If your circle of friends are doing the same things that you are, your circle is too small." Finally, and more importantly, this book reveals a well-kept secret; that there are thousands and thousands of people who have overcome addictions and bad habits to become happy and successful.

What God starts He will finish. If he placed it in you, He will bring it out of you. I believe that. You're not too old. You didn't miss the opportunity. I believe that. God has it all figured out. He knows how to connect the dots. In the Bible, Abraham and Sarah were 100-years-old when God gave them the child He promised. Sarah was barren and unfortunately they went about it the wrong way at first. They thought that God was taking too long, so Sarah told Abraham to have sex with another women. Girl bye! Well he did and of course that didn't go well. But ultimately they did have the child God promised. My point is it's never too late to begin again.

Don't get it twisted you have to fight change. I didn't just stumble into this place, I fought to get here. I stopped blaming other people, forgave myself and the men that used me and took responsibility for myself. I seek out positive women who are where I want to be, and I watch them. Every day I have to encouraged myself to keep moving forward because life will throw punches, but I think of where I once was and quickly remember that I got this. You have to be intentional about living a good life. Ladies, do not think that the good life solely consists of things and stuff, although there is nothing wrong with things. But the life that I am speaking of consists of joy, peace and contentment. You have to believe you are capable and worthy of making the necessary changes to become the woman you want to be. I still dream of more for my life. I also have started a vision board with pictures, positive words or affirmations on it that remind me of where I want to go, what I want to do and who I want to become. I want more and I am being intentional about getting it.

Beautifully CHANGED

If nothing ever changed,
there would be no butterflies.
-Unknown

INTRODUCTION
IF NOTHING CHANGES

If nothing changes, nothing changes. A phrase that I had heard by my counselor during my 30 day stay in my first rehab center. It has taken many years for that statement to take root in my life. I didn't realize then that changing required a decision, and it is work. Changing everything from my thinking and my behavior is necessary, if you want to truly recover from any type of addiction. We can be addicted to many things, ladies—men, money, gambling, pornography reasoning - you name it, it can become your god.

Although I had stopped using drugs during those 30 days, nothing had changed IN me. However, once I made the decision that I had had enough, everything changed. I changed and I wasn't afraid anymore. I have been clean of drugs for twenty years, twenty years, ladies!!

The road has been long and hard. It has been a journey of fighting to take the next step and make good decisions. But I tell you from my heart that every change, every tear, lesson, bad decision and heartache has been worth it. I'm still here. You're still here. The game of life is a forever path of choosing to play. It's a training that never ends, the game just gets easier. I have been rewarded with so much. My story is not a message to make all of your problems disappear. It is a message of God's faithfulness in the midst of the storms of life.

YOU ONLY
HAVE TO BELIEVE

When things don't work out as you hope (trust me sis, they won't), keep believing.

One of my favorite poems by Marianne Williamson describes it perfectly:

Our greatest fear is not that we are inadequate,

but that we are powerful beyond measure.

It is our light, not our darkness that frightens us.

We ask ourselves,

who am I to be brilliant, gorgeous, handsome talented and fabulous?

Actually who are you not to Be?

You are a child of God.

Your playing small does not serve the world.

There is nothing enlightened about shrinking so that other people won't feel insecure around you.

We were born to make manifest the glory of God within us.

It is not just in some; it is in everyone.

And as we let our own light shine,

we consciously give other people permission to do the same.

As we are liberated from our own fear,

our presence automatically liberates others.

SEARCH FOR YOUR
PURPOSE AND DO IT

With this book I have given myself permission to be completely honest with myself so that I can be a blessing to many. I realize that God has been faithful, and I have lived this journey sprinkled with His favor. I fumbled along the path of addiction, lies, manipulation, stealing and low self-esteem for a long time but I count myself blessed that God has prepared me to share my story; and for those that long to change and know Him, something through my life experiences will show them.

I often tell my son that people are looking for answers. I believe that some of those answers are stored up within me. I see so many people filled with fear and needing faith. I still struggle with it, but we all have a choice to make. I say choose LIFE. The fact of the matter is, we have only one life and every decision made matters. There has always been a nudging within, but I ignored it for so long. As I think about it, I was afraid to be anything other than what I was.

I knew that I had a story to tell but I was not completely sure mine really would make a difference. I see so many people who have written books, some of them passionate about the same things that I am—changing lives, but I did not really know how or think that I could be one of those people. So many have already told the story. But then, I thought for a split second, *you know what, I have not told mine.* I was back and forth with myself and a friend asking "What if people did not read my book?" After a few seconds she replied, "What if they do?"

The unknown can be frightening. So one day I made an intelligent decision, just as I had done to get and stay clean, to take a leap of faith and just write; and hopefully inspire other women to realize their own truth, that anything is possible if you only believe.

GRATEFUL
FOR IT ALL

Gratitude is like fuel for the soul. And I make sure that I never run out. How can I? When I look back over my life and see all that God has brought me through, I am eternally grateful. As much as people do not like their circumstances they often are not unhappy enough to change it. With tears streaming down my face, I sat and took inventory of the most disappointing and ugliest times of my life. I was genuinely tired and wanted something better…something meaningful. God had been so good to me. Even after so many awful things that I had done, He still loves me. He loves you too.

I grew up in a single parent household. I never had a relationship with my father. I spent a few summers with him and his parents, but those days were short-lived. We reconnected many years later and although we still don't have a relationship, I have made peace with it. He knows he is loved. I am the middle child of three. I have an older brother and a younger sister. I thoroughly enjoyed my childhood. As a kid, I spent a lot of time outside playing hopscotch, jacks and jump rope. One of my favorite things to do was to play in the rain. When it would flood, we played in the water on flooded streets. Our streets flooded a lot.

I really feel sad for the kids today. They have no clue on what playing outside is. Social media like Facebook, Twitter and Instagram has taken the fun out of being a kid. There is very little personal interaction among kids anymore. Most communication comes through phones or tablets. Now don't throw stones at me. I'm not condemning technology. If any of you follow me on social media you know that I struggle with technology. I have had a laptop and iPhone both which my son gave me, and I am still learning how to use them both. I mean my Apple Mac, girl it is embarrassing not knowing how to navigate around that thing.

As a matter of fact my son convinced me to start writing on my laptop instead of a notebook! But regardless of the side comments and behind my back gossip about my lack of knowledge regarding technology, I'm going to keep going, keep asking for help and keep learning. One thing that I've come to realize about me is that I can do whatever I put my mind to.

Anyway, I'm simply saying that the fun of being a kid seems extinct. Today it seems to be hard work being a kid, keeping up with wearing the right clothes, having the right hairstyle and the right phone! Its constant peer pressure brought on by magazines and rap videos. And the bullying is terrible. Ugh, do not get me started with that. They don't have what I did growing up, playing kickball, hide and go seek, playing in the creek and climbing trees. There was also the Boys and Girls Club where we played basketball, game room we played pool, ping pong and went swimming. Most of us neighborhood kids would go there after school because it was a good place to gather and have fun. There were also different activities that we could sign up for if we wanted to. Everyone in the community would often gather there because Huntington is not a very big city. Everyone knew each other. On Saturdays you could count on the entire community being at the football field all day. The saying "It takes a village..." holds true, back when I was growing up.

Now, all we can do is be the example to our kids, mentor them and teach them the importance of making good choices, integrity and love. I was a midget league cheerleader for about three years. The team you were on depended pretty much on your age. As I sit here thinking back to that particular time, I can't help but smile. There really was a village of folks that cheered you on and at the same time would whoop your butt if you did something wrong, call your momma and when you made it to the house you were whooped again.

Another special time growing up was going to Myrtle Beach with my family. That's where my love of the beach comes from. I still love going there. I actually make it a point to go to Myrtle Beach every year. It's only a four-hour drive so I can get there and hang out, even just for a long weekend. Myrtle Beach has changed drastically but the memories of being there have not. My grandmother and grandfather took us almost every year. Sometimes we went to Six Flags in Florida. It was so exciting to see my grandmother packing our clothes and buying and packing food to go on vacation. And the thought of going on vacation, packing clothes and food still excites me. In any case, we would stop frequently to use the rest room, eat and stretch our legs. Stopping also gave my grandparents a break from our constant asking, "are we there yet?"

We would stop in Charlotte, NC to eat breakfast at Shoney's, then we would stop at a rest area to eat lunch. My grandmother packed enough food for all of us, for an entire week because the resort we stayed at had a kitchen. She had a menu for every day.

I actually have picked up a lot of her qualities, from vacation planning and packing to reading and house cleaning. I never mastered her cooking skills and man, she could cook. One of my favorite dishes of hers was liver and onions. She also made the best freaking pineapple upside-down cake. Yum!!!! Sundays were memorable days for me. We went to a Catholic church and I remained in the Catholic faith until I became an adult. I decided to get baptized as a Baptist at the age of 22. After church, we would eat dinner at my grandparents' house.

Sundays were definitely a day of rest, back then. Nothing was open except a gas station and one convenience store like 7-eleven. You spent time with your family having dinner together at the table actually talking to each other. Afterwards, we watched television, took a nap or sat on the porch and talked with neighbors. I definitely give big kudos to Chick-fil-A and Hobby Lobby for being closed on Sundays. They stand firm on their beliefs, allow their employees that day off. Ugh, I miss those Sundays.

GETTING PAST
YOUR PAST

It would be 20 years before my family got together for another beach trip. When my grandmother passed away from cancer so much seemed to change with our family. She was no doubt the glue and once we lost her we came apart. Although distance has played a part, none of us are as close as we used to be. Most of us live in the same city, but even that doesn't seem to matter. We rarely see each other. Work, kids and other commitments can make it hard to find the time to get together; but the truth is people make time for what's important to them. Excuses can disguise themselves in a variety of different ways. I am definitely guilty of making excuses for not spending time with my family. I mean, once I get off of work, I just want to go home and put on my pajamas. I tell myself that I've worked 10 hours on my feet; and saying that somehow would excuse me from the truth——that it wasn't important.

See ladies, we make time for what we want to make time for. If we wanna get our feet done, we make time to do it. Nails and hair did, no problem. There is a hard truth that I'm not quite sure many of us believe and that is time waits on no one. So often, we think we have time; but any time wasted is time that we cannot get back. Over the last couple of years, I feel like our family is making small steps to gather together more. I'm making an effort to have everyone over a couple times a month, and if everyone shows it is usually thirteen of us. Everyone pitches in and brings a dish. They know that come 9 or 10 o'clock, its over because that is my bedtime and I usually don't deviate from it. Sleep is important to me and I function better when I get rest.

I became a thief at a very early age. I attended St. Joseph, a Catholic school during grades 1-3. I don't remember much about those years; but I do remember that every Wednesday I went to mass, and I and my best friend dressed alike just about every day. Before the start of each school year until 3rd grade her mom would take us school shopping and every outfit matched. The 3rd grade also marked the start of a bad habit for me of stealing. I stole a broach from my grandmother. Omg did she put a whoopin to my backside. I gave the broach to my 3rd grade teacher, Mrs. Ally. Once Mrs. Ally realized I stole it, she returned it my grandmother. Although that gesture was good and thoughtful, it wasn't mine to give and it wasn't the right thing to do.

Unfortunately I didn't learn my lesson. I continued to steal for many years after that. No worries, ladies, I will share all the dirt with you about my days of theft in the upcoming chapters. But by God's grace, I have never been arrested for stealing. Another reason I know that God watched over and kept me all these years. When I started elementary school at Simms, which ran from grades 1-6, I liked it right away. By the end of 6th grade I knew every teacher, hallway and chalkboard. I also knew most of the kids. The years at Simms were what they should be for kids—fun, friends and the start of liking boys. When I think about it, it's funny how a crush on a boy tickled my fancy. The innocence of it all. There was no pressure. You just wrote on a piece of paper "I like you Do you like me? Check yes or no." That was it, really. If he checked yes that meant y'all went together.

I had a couple boys that I liked in elementary school. {Laughing} I also remember even liking my 6th grade teacher, Mr. Woods. He was fine. As a matter of fact, all the girls in my 6th grade class liked him. We would all get mad when we would see him talking to other female teachers. Mr. Woods was well liked in our class. He cared and he showed it.

In Junior High School, I soared in athletics. I was the captain of the cheerleaders, basketball, volleyball and track teams. During my 7th grade year I began to develop close friendships with a lot of my classmates. There were different clubs that you could participate in, but I never joined any of them because my time was tied up in sports. Pep rallies were one of my favorite events, especially during football season. We were allowed to wear our cheerleading uniforms to school.

It wasn't long before I became popular among my classmates. I also started dating. I was in 8th grade when I started dating a 9th grader. He was captain of the football team so that validated me even more with my classmates. He and I knew each other from the community that we lived in. Most of the blacks that went to Lincoln Jr. High lived within a few blocks of each other. We all walked to school together, most of the time. If you lived in Huntington WV you pretty much knew everyone, and everyone knew you.

Today, knowing your neighbors isn't so common anymore. People don't seem interested in knowing you and you are more than likely not interested in knowing them. I lost my virginity while in 8th grade to the football guy that I was dating. I liked him a lot and I wanted to be with him. He was my first kiss, my first love, my first everything. We didn't use protection and I knew to use a condom. I had already been given the speech from my mother about the birds and the bees.

Sure enough I ended up pregnant at the age of thirteen. Not sure how my grandmother knew I was pregnant, but she did. When my mother was pregnant with my brother, my great grandmother knew she was pregnant too. Mother denied it up until she was about seven months, but grandma knew. When grandmother asked me, I immediately said no because I was afraid of her knowing that I had been sexually active. She didn't believe me, and the doctor visit confirmed that I was indeed pregnant. My mother was informed, and they decided abortion was the answer. I was too young. It was a very emotional time for me. I didn't have a say in whether or not I was keeping the baby, so I had an abortion. My boyfriend and his mother were informed but only my grandmother and me went together to have the procedure. And I cried for days. I knew my grandmother was disappointed, but she never made me feel like I was a disappointment.

I did not miss a lot of school after the abortion. I remember walking through the halls of our school and seeing classmates having the best time. They were standing in groups talking. Couples were holding hands. But I felt unworthy, guilty and ashamed. I was just existing, really, not fully engaged at all. Slowly I somehow dug myself out of the black hole that my thoughts had dug me into. I still was in and out of a relationship with the guy that I had the abortion for, but he started dating another girl.

She and I never really had words, but there was tension among us. She also went to our school. She and I both would go over to his house and it was like we both were ok with him seeing us both. Talk about low self-esteem. After they both left junior high to go to high school, she ended up getting pregnant and had the baby. From then on, I did not see him much unless we were hanging out at the boys' club or hanging out on the block.

The block on 16th street was where you could really find anything you wanted—parked cars and music, weed, pills, boosters selling all kinds of items that they has stolen from the department store. You name it, you could always find it on the block. But I never dealt with the pain from the abortion or from feeling like I was rejected. I stuffed every emotion that surfaced. I started smoking cigarettes and dating a couple of other guys. I had my first encounter with a white guy while in junior high. We were never sexually active. Growing our relationship was hard because it had to be kept a secret from his parents because I was black. Needless to say, the relationship faded away.

I continued with sports and made it through 9th grade with an average GPA at best. Leaving junior high was exciting and sad. We were all going our separate ways. There were two high schools in the area, and it seemed that whites went to one, blacks the other. Although we tried to stay in touch, being at different schools, time was not on our side and eventually we lost contact. I received a message about two years ago letting me know that our junior high school coach had passed away. It took me back to those years in school when it was just good.

High school was a lot different for me. I didn't play any sports and a part of me felt like I did not fit in. I did not feel popular anymore. It was not long after getting to the 10th grade that I started smoking pot. My mom sold it as a

19

side hustle so I would steal it pretty often. We mostly walked to school as we did in junior high and my friends and I would get high before school started. A lot of days we skipped school and hung out at a friend's house who was older than us. As a matter of fact a lot of people hung out there.

Our friend loved to cook, and he could cook his butt off. His house became the spot where people would go to smoke, eat, play cards and listen to music. The entire three years of high school I did not apply myself at all. I did what was necessary to barely get by. I started going to the clubs, hanging out with girlfriends at the college campus, sleeping with older men for money and stealing from them, if the opportunity presented itself. Men often told men how pretty I was, and I used my looks to get a lot of free stuff from them—jewelry, pot, clothes and money. But how many of y'all know it was not for free? There is always a cost and a consequence {good or bad} for our decisions and my decisions cost me. I ended up getting gonorrhea from one guy that I slept with and crabs from another. Fortunately both were STDs that were treatable and curable. From then on, I promised myself that I would always keep condoms in my purse.

IT IS
WHAT IT IS

I graduated in 1985 and not long after graduation I ended up dating and committing to a guy that I had known growing up. He lived in Logan WV, which is about an hour and a half from Huntington. He lived there with his mom and siblings—three sisters and a brother. Our families knew each other, so dating him was not surprising. He played basketball in Huntington a lot and he pretty much knew everyone. Remember, Huntington is not a very big city.

I would often steal my mother's car in the middle of the night to go see him while he attended WV State. I would see him at least once a week and he would also come to visit me as well. After a while we agreed to dating only each other so we did not use condoms after that. I ended up getting pregnant…again. He and I talked about the pregnancy, spoke with our mothers about it and decided that we would keep the baby. After he graduated from college, he decided to go into the Air Force. I didn't see him for six weeks; but after basic training, he came home. His first stop was to see his mom, then me. He was home only for a short time before he had to leave to go to Kuwait. We made a trip to Logan to see his family for a few days. We spoke at least once a month and he would always say that he loved and missed us. I missed him. I never had to set up for any child support with social services because he sent money every month. If we needed or wanted anything he would send it.

I don't exactly remember how long he was in Kuwait, but he came home on another brief leave before he had to go to Hawaii. We made another trip to Logan to see his family, then back home. We talked about Brandon and me going with him. We shared our thoughts with my mother and she immediately said no. She said I was too young, and Brandon was too little. Neither of us made a big fuss because we knew she was right. I had help staying home.

We continued to date for a year or so after our son was born and then decided to part ways. The distance drew us apart but even after we split up, we remained friends. Even today after parenting our son of 35 years, we still say I love you to each other.

I decided to go to beauty school soon after graduation. I knew I didn't want to go to college. Hair and makeup was something that I had always been interested in and I was good at them both. While in school I colored my hair often. Haircolor is fun and formulating color and makeup application was something I excelled at. My mother, sister and my grandparents were a huge help babysitting while I was in beauty school. I went five days a week and completed my course in a year. I graduated and started working in a full-service salon. Although I had done well in beauty school, working in a salon was completely different. There were no instructors there to help you to navigate services. I had a lot to learn.

I never really felt like I was a single mom because I gratefully had help from family. Actually I was able to still hang out with my girlfriends, go to the club and pretty much do what I wanted because someone was always available to take care of Brandon. However, because I did still live at home, me and my mother often bumped heads about how I raised Brandon and what I could and could not do while living in her house. I remember one day she and I were

23

arguing about a guy that I was seeing. He was older and a street hustler, so my mother didn't like him. She went on and on about how he was no good, he had a girlfriend and that he sold drugs. Back and forth we went. Finally she said, "don't say another word." Well I wanted her to hear what I had to say. Firmly she said, "bitch I said don't say another word." Well of course I had to get the last word in and before I knew it she had hit me in the head with an iron cast skillet. I ended up getting ten stiches in my head.

Now, if that was to happen today, parents would be in jail. Sometimes I think that is part of the reason kids are disrespectful towards their parents because all you have to do is claim abuse and you will be arrested. I've even seen situations where the parent actually seemed scared of the child. I was cutting this kids hair and I immediately could tell he didn't want a haircut. He plopped down in my chair and his mother came over to tell me how to cut his hair. The boy, who was about 11 or 12 years of age said to her, "would you shut up and sit down." I was beyond disbelief. Do you know what she did? She shut up and sat down!!! Wow right?

DONT RUN FROM
FACING THE TRUTH

I got my first apartment. I had been on a waiting list for Section 8, for a while and an opportunity opened up. I was so ready to get out of my mother's house and do what I wanted and see who I wanted in my own place. It was a two-bedroom, living room, one bath and kitchen. It was perfect and right on the bus line. My best friend ended up getting an apartment right across from me, so we were thrilled. She had a daughter a few months younger than my son, so the kids played together a lot.

Having my own place was wonderful. I decorated it the way I wanted. I have always been a big fan of Goodwill stores. You can find good bargains there, so it was easy to make my place feel like home. My grandmother and mom helped me to get bigger items like beds and a kitchen table. I am also a huge lover of plants and I made sure I had plenty. Some of my friends and I would often go out in the middle of the night and steal plants off of porches. Some were often too big to carry but we managed to get them without being caught. A lot of mornings before work my girlfriend and I would often talk outside on the balcony about what we were going to do after work. We both received food stamps, so we would grocery shop together. Remember the books of food stamps? Seems like everyone that received them back then sold some. You would give $25 cash and get $50 in stamps, Stop playing, y'all remember. Anyway, we both stayed in the apartments for about three years until we both decided we need a bigger place. The kids were getting bigger. We had accumulated more and more stuff. It was time. Another opportunity opened with Section 8 for a bigger place and we both ended up moving. This time we were not neighbors, but we still hung out together a lot.

My real father has never embraced me. I used to wonder why. Definitely not having a father around could be one of the reasons why I used to be so promiscuous with men. I mean that's what therapists say—that I was looking for love. But I don't try to figure it out anymore. I have forgiven him. We often think that forgiving means that we approve of what a person did. Naw, it just means we are choosing to rise above what is and find peace. One thing's for sure, he has missed out on seeing me become a beautiful woman as well as missing out on knowing his grandson. I reached out to him and invited him to my 50th birthday gathering, and he came. You know what, it wasn't awkward for me. I had forgiven him a long time ago. I was incredibly happy that he came. We don't talk much... neither one of us really know what to say... but it's all good. I feel like we both now love each other.

My grandfather took the place of a father to me, for the most part. I suppose that is why I called him daddy. He recently passed away from stomach cancer. I got to spend a lot of time with him during the years prior to him passing, so I am grateful for the time together. He has always provided for his family. We all benefited from his work at the steel mill and at the hotel. As kids, we would be so excited to get in the car and go get him from work. We would fight over who was going to sit in the front seat. We would pick him up from the steel mill and take him down the street to the hotel where he worked as a bell boy. Most of the grandkids call him daddy I think because he was the father figure for us. The great grands call him granddaddy.

Daddy was also a drug dealer. He sold pills at first, then cocaine, and eventually crack. He was involved with a whorehouse and a white woman for years. Although I can't image the fear, anger and low self-worth my grandmother felt about my grandfather's lifestyle, she chose to stay with him. She chose every day to accept and spend the money that came from selling drugs; even when my grandfather went to prison, three times, she stayed. She loved him and no matter how dysfunctional their relationship was, one thing was evident, their love for each other. Although they had 5 children, only 2 of them were actually my grandfather's. He took care of us all. My grandmother grew up as a child of an alcoholic mother. I often wondered if even she was suffering from low self-esteem and rejection from her childhood. My great grandmother was an alcoholic. I remember, as a little girl sitting on the liquor house porch with her often. I liked being with her. Even though she drank, she was my grandma and I loved her. She would give me a quarter to go down the street to Mr. Davis' grocery store. Back in the day, a quarter could get you a few pieces of candy. It was a small grocery that served our community for years. Sometimes, Mr. Davis would allow grandma to get a few items and pay him the following week. I'm not sure but I suspect he did that for a lot of people. He was a good man. Years later grandma got sober and took on another habit of chewing tobacco. Her favorite was apple and I didn't mind getting it for her when she asked me to. Grandma passed away in 1990 in a nursing home, at the age of 86.

WHAT THE DEVIL MEANT FOR EVIL
GOD WILL USE FOR GOOD

I continued to work as a stylist and really things were going well. Brandon was growing up so fast. I loved my apartment. We lived right across the street from Marshall University football stadium. I didn't go to many football games, but Huntington was and still is a football city. It was always fun to sit on my porch and watch people walk to the stadium and hear the intercom of all the plays and happenings during the game. I started selling a little bit of weed and cocaine on the side. My mom had a hustle in selling weed and I would often steal it from her to make extra cash for myself. Back in the day people would look to purchase joints and I had them. Somehow I noticed that She kept it hidden under her dresser in the bedroom and when she was downstairs or in the bathroom I would get a small amount because I didn't want her to think any was missing. A friend of mine would score weed from my mom too and it wasn't long after that he started to sell cocaine for my mom and that is basically how I started using crack. You see, I started hanging out with him. It all started casually, but my addiction would soon come full--term after a couple of years.

I started socially getting high until somewhere along the line I became dependent on using every day. I started spending every extra dollar I had on getting high. When I didn't have the money I would call up a few men who I knew from the street and exchange sex for money. I never considered myself a prostitute because I never walked the streets, but the practice was still the same. I was caught up in the grips of the disease of addiction and for the next year or so using became necessary for survival. I exchanged sexual favors to be able to get the money I needed to get high. After countless tries to stop using and get myself together I had no choice but to leave WV. My grandmother had already sold our childhood home and moved to Charlotte. She had become mentally and emotionally tired of my grandfather's lifestyle. My aunt took an opportunity to go, as well. They both agreed that I wasn't able to be a mother, so Brandon went with them. Sometimes, even when you know you're in desperate conditions, convincing yourself that you have lost control isn't that easy.

I sought a cure by geographic change. I thought if I just got out of Huntington I would be ok. And I was for a while until I realized that in order for anything to change in my life, I first had to change. It wasn't where I lived or who was in my life that would keep me clean…I had to decide I wanted to stay clean. I HAD TO develop a sense of self-worth and learn self-respect. I had to believe that I was worthy of a better life.

I relocated to Pittsburgh where my mom had moved a couple years earlier. She had to leave WV, as well, because had she not left, she most likely would have ended up in jail. I stayed clean for eight years. Life was going great. I still worked as a stylist. I joined Narcotics Anonymous, met a very special group of good people who had similar stories of addiction just like me and were able to stay clean, got a sponsor and continued practicing the traditions and steps of NA where addicts help other addicts. It's very aspiring to see. Together, one by one, everyone wins. I was very grateful for the gift of recovery. My life had become manageable. I focused a lot on my spiritual growth, worked to get a better perspective of my life and just enjoyed being clean. One night at a meeting with my sponsor I met a guy that I ended up dating for eight years. I had seen him a time or two before in the same meeting. I inquired about him to my sponsor and she felt that I was far enough into my sobriety that having a friend wouldn't hurt. Getting involved too soon during the early stages of recovery could end in relapse if you hadn't worked on yourself first. She introduced us and we immediately hit it off. He had been clean for a few years before we met, and it wasn't long before we started hanging out going to meetings together.

I finally introduced him to my mom and to Brandon, and they both liked him. His family lived about an hour from Pittsburgh and I was introduced to them as well. They didn't mind that I had a son (he didn't have children) and we visited his family pretty often. A lot of Sundays we would drive to see his family, have dinner and spend most of the day. His sister lived in the area and she had three children close to Brandon's age. We soon decided to be exclusive and after a year of dating and focusing on our sobriety, we decided to get a small one-bedroom apartment right around the corner from where my mother lived. Brandon would stay at my mom's most of the time but often he would stay with us. The elementary school that he attended was in walking distance so between me, mom and my boyfriend it was easy for one of us to get him to and from school.

Recovery was good. Our relationship was going well. We eventually ended up moving to the north side of Pittsburgh and was able to get a bigger apartment. Brandon was able to walk to school with some of the kids in the neighborhood that he became friends with. Some days I would walk with him. One day, while walking him to school I noticed a church on the corner that had a 6am prayer service daily. That was right up my alley because I was a morning person. Getting up early to have coffee and read my meditation books had become a habit and incorporating prayer would be perfect. So every morning I would drive down the street at 5:50am and sit and pray. To my surprise, there were always at least six to a dozen people there. Being there made such a difference in my day. I continued to go for 2 years. There was also a midget league football team that we were able to get Brandon on and he played for a couple years. That first year was tough for me because he was my baby and the first time he got hit in practice, I thought, *nope he cannot play football*. His coach laughed when I shared my concerns, but he assured me that he would be fine. One football game, Brandon was on his way to scoring a touchdown and I ran all the way down the field with him until he was tackled. We laughed about that for a long time. I mean hey, I was a proud momma seeing him getting ready to score.

We started accumulating more stuff and saving money. We spent 8 years together and I never knew something was changing. I mean, relationships have their challenges and I thought we worked through them, but something happened, and I could sense something was different. He started staying out later, didn't want me going to the meetings with him anymore, saying he was going with the guys. One night after coming in from eating dinner I felt in my spirit that he was on the phone with a female. Ladies, we have intuition. Most of the time we know. We sense things. So I went upstairs and quietly picked up the phone in our bedroom and it confirmed what I felt. I confronted him and of course put him out. The only things I allowed him to leave with were his clothes. I was devastated. I was hurt. I was angry. My sponsor helped me get through it…eventually. But not until after I keyed his car and made a couple appearances to his apartment when I knew he had company. It was tough. I can remember all of the old feelings of inadequacy and low self-esteem surface.

LET YOUR MESS
BECOME YOUR MESSAGE

To fill the void and ease the pain I got into a relationship with my son's football coach. We both were on the rebound. He had gotten divorced a year or so earlier and was casually dating at the time. We continued to see each other regularly(and secretly) for about six months. He didn't want anyone to know because of him being Brandon's coach. But I knew better. He was seeing another one of his football players mother's. Again ladies, we just know.

Our relationship was short-lived. I mean, there was never a commitment, only convenience. I had an opportunity to move into a new community of town homes. They were so nice! My very first new home. Brandon and I had lived in apartments but never a brand-new home. Brandon was not too happy to move. He liked being close to his best friend, who lived on the north side. He stayed over our house pretty often and Brandon stayed at his house, even more. But it was a great opportunity. A brand-new townhome in a brand-new community.

I got new furniture and I really liked the fact that we had access to downtown Pittsburgh. We could literally walk downtown in a few minutes. I was so proud of what I had accomplished. I even purchased a car, my very first car. I was happy. I was proud. It seemed as though I had found peace within. It seemed as though I was on my way to forgiveness of self and others. Although I had a lot of work still to do in my recovery, I was happy with where I was heading. I continued to work as a stylist and after a few months the townhouse was fully furnished.

I remember riding down the street one day, heading home from my mom's house and noticed a block where, as an addict, you know drugs are sold. For weeks, I would go that way just checking things out, not even realizing I was already in a mental relapse. Entertaining the thought of using is very dangerous. Staying away from people, places and things is critical. I knew it. In the rooms of NA they tell you that.

After eight years of sobriety, I used. I'm not sure what caused me to ruin it all…arrogance…but I did.

At first, for months I could handle it. I still paid all of my bills. I still went to work. I wasn't running the streets or selling my body. I befriended a drug dealer so he would bring me the product, or I would drive to him and pick the product up. I did such a great job pretending that I was still clean, but my life was slowly spinning out of control. I stopped going to meetings. I gradually stopped calling my sponsor. My life was really all kinds of screwed up. I just wanted to see but didn't see it.

Ultimately, I lost everything. Again. It's amazing how much further down ROCK BOTTOM can get.

I remember two particular events: One was letting a drug dealer have a key to my house and I didn't have any regard to how Brandon felt. The other was selling our TV and microwave and telling Brandon they broke and had to be fixed. But he knew the truth. He never said anything about anything, but I know he was hurt and embarrassed and scared. Oh, my car was totaled by a drug dealer and the sad thing was when he knocked on the door to tell me my car was down the street, axle hanging off, instead of going to get my car, I waited about 30 minutes because I wanted to get high. I was afraid to call my mom, so I waited a few hours until I came down from my high.

We ended up losing the townhouse. Everything that I owned was set on the street because we were evicted, and the sheriff was called to padlock the door. That was the day my mom found out that I was using again. I had lost control of my life again and I was too proud to ask for help. I had gotten letters and a couple of times I was able to come up with the money. All of our belongings were on the curb of the street because I was ashamed to tell mom weeks before that I had gotten an eviction notice. In my mind I thought that some kind of way I could fix the situation. Needless to say, I couldn't. We put everything in storage, but I couldn't pay the monthly fee because I ended up losing my job and continued to use. I ended up losing it all. Brandon's toys, pictures of him as a baby—everything. We had to move in with my mom and stepfather.

Even when I think about it today, I still feel pain—not really for the stuff but— for Brandon. He has endured so much heartache and embarrassment. I even remember times of smoking crack while Brandon laid next to me in the bed. We often slept together to keep him from having to sleep on the couch. I feel he had to hear me flicking the lighter. He has never mentioned it. But I think he knew. For years I stayed stuck in guilt and shame about things I did and who I was. Guilt and shame ate away at me, depressed me. I felt empty and forced false happiness many times. But I'm so glad that I took my place among those that are living the good life. The forgiven and the freed. And sis if you sometimes feel the way I did, consumed by guilt and shame, hold on. If you are willing to do the work, you won't feel this way forever. You will have to dig deep but it will be well worth it.

I missed birthdays and Christmases due to my addiction. Thank God for my mom who did everything she could to keep my son as stable and happy as she could. She thought putting him in counseling would help him to release his anger and frustrations. I recommend counseling to anyone who just needs an ear to hear. Sometimes we don't need answers we need to let it all out and through the process of talking answers come. I went to visit my counselor once a week. I don't think he liked talking about his feelings. Most of us don't. It's painful. I mean to share all of my failures in this book is painful. Writing has brought up so many feelings of guilt and shame. There are so many regrets. I don't really know if counseling helped my son. Truth is y'all, I have never asked him. I hope somewhere deep down that it did.

After cycling in and out three treatment centers, Narcotics Anonymous and counseling, I still was not ready to change. Mom did everything she could to help out with making sure that my son and I would be ok. I spent many a days in the crack house. I wouldn't bathe or brush my teeth for days. All of your standards fly out the door when you are getting high. You start hanging out with people you normally wouldn't. You become the person that you probably would avoid being drug free. One of the crack houses that I stayed in had no water so when I had to use the bathroom the toilet was filled with bowels and urine. I tried to stay in the living room, which was the cleanest part of the house. Drug dealers would come in and out, occasionally leaving large amounts of crack to the couple who lived there as a way of saying thanks for letting them use their houses to cook up, bag up and sell crack cocaine. Most of the time they would share with me since I was there. After days of being gone I would finally call, and mom would let me come home. My son would look so sad, hardly saying anything to me at all. Inside, I was dying because I know I messed up. After a few days of rest and trying to be a good mom I would be gone again.

Nothing seemed to help, and my mom was out of suggestions and patience. She ended up calling my son's father who lived in Las Vegas. My son went to spend his high school years with his dad. Turned out that it was the best move for him. The only, and last, option it seemed was a two-year program. The others hadn't worked for me. Intervention didn't help. Seeing the pain I had caused my son hadn't helped me to stay clean. I was completely in the grips of my addiction. So my sister and my best friend took me to a two-year program in Durham, North Carolina. It was called Trosa. I packed up a lot of clothes because I wanted to look good. I was good at dressing up the outside. My hair was always done. I didn't look like a crack head, but believe me, I was.

GOD'S
PERFECT TIMING

Everything that happened up until the day that I was dropped off at Trosa told the story that I was a liar, a thief, selfish and manipulative. THE THREE OTHER TREATMENT CENTERS SERVED ONLY AS 30-day TEMPORARY RESTING PLACES. I stayed clean, of course, got some basic tools to use to help with my sobriety like learning techniques of meditation and journaling (both are still very instrumental in my daily routine); but I didn't address any inward issues. Trosa would change all that.

Upon entering, I wasn't able to have anything that I brought with me; no clothes, no jewelry. No make-up. They gave me everything I needed. The program would break and humble me. I didn't want to stay. Who were they to tell me what I could wear!? But they knew, first and foremost, that a person could not truly get and stay clean unless they take an honest look at their life and admit how out of control it really was. The mask had to come off. The true you, just as you are, was to be exposed. I did not like it. My sister begged me to stay and for them to keep me there. Reluctantly, after 30 minutes of trying to negotiate with them to let me keep my things, I stayed. I really didn't have a choice because I had abused every living situation, so I had nowhere else to go.

My first 30 days consisted of cleaning floors, walls and cooking. I lived in a house with 20 women, four to a room. I couldn't do anything but clean, eat and go to meetings. I wasn't able to talk to any men and they couldn't talk to me. Every morning I had to get up and shower early because the water wouldn't be hot later. I had to cook breakfast for the other women, get dressed in the clothes they provided and clean until it was time to eat dinner. I felt so angry. I didn't understand the strategy of the program. Sixty days without a relaxer or make-up? Ugh!! And now I seldom wear make-up at all. Even when I am working, my make-up regime is very light…mascara and lipstick. I made it through 30 days and the entire program celebrated with you that you made it through. It was hard. I made some friends and the next 30 days were better.

I still didn't want to be there, but I didn't have anywhere else to go. My mom and sister made it clear that I couldn't come back until I finished the program. I was able to have a little more privileges like watch tv with the other ladies in the house. Ninety days in, I was able to put a relaxer in my hair. Things had definitely gotten better. I had a lot more freedom. I still wasn't able to talk to men. That part of the program was so that we women could focus on ourselves. I didn't like it because history said men validated me. But I understood it. Recovery meant more than just not using drugs. It was an internal change that had to take place. God has given me a heart for women and I truly believe that there at Trose is where I felt my calling. It wasn't hard to develop a bond with the women in the house. We had so much in common; drug addiction, loss, low self-esteem, liars and thieves. It was there that I realize the roots addictions run deep. I grew up in a family where using drugs was normal. But I didn't want that to be my legacy.

One morning after breakfast, a few of us were sitting at the kitchen table reading the Bible and talking. Now don't get it twisted, I'm not a Bible scholar, by no means, but there are so many stories in the Bible that I can relate to. One in particular is about the woman with the issue of blood. She heard Jesus was coming to town and she knew if she could touch the hem of his garment, she would be made whole. She wasn't ready to die. She had known on the inside that she was far from dead. Nothing in her life said healing... whole... renew... forgiven... loved. But, she believed anyway. Have you ever had a moment, an awakening, if you will, where something inside you just stood up and said, "I am better than this, I know who I am. I am a mother, an author, a leader." It was at that precise moment that I knew I wouldn't use drugs anymore. I decided to leave the program.

One day, sitting in the office of the program there was a group that had come to tour the Trosa campus. After my 30 days of successful assessment I was offered a job in the front office strictly working for the president of the treatment center. My job was to answer the phones, set up the conference room with fresh bagels and donuts and assist with whatever he needed me to do. Once the visitors arrived they had to check in at the front office. After their tour of Trosa they had to check out and most of the time leave forwarding information for graduates of the Trosa.

A few months later, I contacted a ministry program for men to see if there was any room for me there, or if they possibly had a women's ministry. The women and the counselor at Trosa encouraged me to finish the program, but there was a deep knowing in my spirit that knew I had had enough. And just like the Bible story, the woman with the issue of blood, I knew. I believed that if I could only get a touch, a closer walk with him, I would be ok. What I have come to know is that it's not what others say about you, but rather what you say about yourself. I would look in the mirror and say over and over to myself, "Missy you get to decide what kind of woman you will be."

I was sat down by counselors because they felt like I was rebelling against the program. I was put on restriction, but I survived the stares and gossip. You know what, sis, believe me when I tell you it is so freeing when you can embrace your decisions, even when people don't understand. I have learned you don't have to have other people's permission to go after what you want. I knew I needed a public healing for all to see so that I could share my story with other women so that they could find their courage too. Trosa is an amazing place to recover. It will humble you. Challenge you. The program has help many of addicts to get on their feet. I mean, heck, once you finish with the program they helped you with employment and housing. However, for the entire two years I wasn't willing to stay. I knew something bigger was waiting for me.

I had written a letter to the ministry and told them of my desire to leave and that I felt a recovery program that would help me get a closer relationship with God is where I needed to be. Remember, in early chapters I mentioned how the program of Narcotics Anonymous gave me a spiritual foundation; so getting back to the basics is where I felt most drawn. So I left the program after six months. I was picked up by the Rev. He was the founder of the program. The ride was a bit quiet, but he assured me that I would be ok. We arrived in Baltimore where the Exodus Men's Ministry was. It was a Christian halfway house for men who were just out of prison to help them find stable housing, jobs and a relationship with God. My family had no idea that I had even considered leaving or that I had left. I think I was there a few weeks before I let them know where I was.

It was in Baltimore that I met a woman who would be very instrumental in my recovery and with my relationship with God. She took me under her wing and poured into me until I was strong enough to be on my own. Her guidance and her passion for God kept me holding on. She was very instrumental in a men's halfway house. She had a passion for black men. She was tough on them, but she was loved. I stayed with her a few months until a room upstairs above the ministry office was cleaned out for me. The men's halfway house was across the street. Reverend had a passion for helping black men fresh out of prison get their life back on track. I felt like I had six big brothers looking after me. Sister Robinson was good to us all, but we had to follow the rules. And going to church was not an option.

I started to notice, after a few months, as I helped out with the organizing of files, and grocery shopping for the men's house that things weren't as they seemed. Rev. began making flirtatious remarks. He often wanted to kiss me. Since I lived upstairs over the office, he would often pop up after hours. When I was in the shower, he would just walk in, pretending that he wanted to tell me what needed to be done in the office that day. I'm amazed and appalled by the preachers and pastors of the world that use their power for less than righteous reasons. I had already made up my mind when I left Trosa that I had one agenda—to soar! So I proposed in my heart to get a job and make a plan to get my own apartment. I got my license renewed and started working as a stylist for Great Clips.

I soon realized that the foodstamps that were supposed to come into the ministry for the men living in the house were going to another household of Rev's choosing. He was dating a girl that ran a similar ministry and they both were abusing government funds and foodstamps. I confronted him, but he denied it. I was so aggravated, and I literally hated being around him but I didn't have anywhere to go. I lived upstairs in the office for another month, putting up with the advances and helping out with whatever needed to be done for the ministry. I got attached to the men. They became like my big brothers; I mean I was the only girl there. I hung out with them when I wasn't working, sitting on the porch, cooking dinner or walking to the corner store.

One night, while sitting on the porch, I recalled the sermon at church that day about the man by the pool for thirty-eight years. Jesus asked him, "wilt thou be made whole?" The man was handicapped, so at first I didn't get it, Why would Jesus asked him that, of course he wanted to be well. I mean who really wants to be crippled? But pastor explained that, although the man was crippled, he could have rolled himself into the water instead of waiting for someone to pick him up. Jesus was saying GET UP! DO SOMETHING ABOUT YOUR CONDITION! Stop blaming other people for not doing what you can do for yourself. So I did just that. I stopped blaming my life on other people, the fact that I grew up in the projects, didn't know my dad, my mom and grandfather sold drugs, my grandma was an alcoholic, I had an abortion at thirteen, slept with men for money, lied and stole. I was ready to be made whole. I had been clean a short while and although I purposed in my heart to stay clean, I was merely surviving. It wasn't enough anymore. This time I was ready.

STEP OUT
AND FIND OUT

I eventually separated the ministry. An apartment opened up for me through a reference from a lady at the church we attended. I was able to save my first three paychecks to move, get some second-hand furniture and fully furnish the apartment. It was a small two bedroom, but totally cute!

The guys in the house helped me move. We all stayed in contact for a while. I still attended the church where we went while I was in the ministry, but I worked a lot, so I didn't see them much after that. I heard a couple of them had a relapse. I'm not sure if the ministry even exists anymore.

If you know anything about Maryland, you know it snows! I remember so many walks in the snow to get to the bus stop to get to work; I caught two buses to get to work and two buses to get home. Carrying groceries in the snow was not fun and to top it all off, I lived four blocks from the bus stop. It was so cold one day and about six inches of snow. Once I made it to my apartment I spent about 10 minutes sitting on my couch before I was warm enough to get my shoes off. It was that cold!

I was able to buy a car after about a year. My credit wasn't that good, so they beat me over the head with the payment. But I had a car and it made a world of difference for me. I'm not knocking riding the bus by any means, but girl, it was rough at times.

After two years in Baltimore I reconnected with a childhood friend. We talked on the phone often and eventually I invited him to visit me. Since we had known each other for years growing up it was really nice to see him and reminisce about our family and other people that we had grown up with. He invited me to Kentucky to visit and I really liked it. He was well established, had a beautiful home and my company salon Great Clips wasn't far from his house. I thought, hmmmm. We continued to visit each other, and he asked me to move in with him. Relocating wasn't in my plan at all, but we got along and a part of me was ready to be in a relationship. What I realize is that I didn't have that knowing me within before I said yes. Yup, I moved. I should have taken heed of the red flag when he told me, soon after packing the truck that I couldn't take my cats.

Initially, he said I could. I ended up just leaving them a nearby church with their food and water bowl and toys. I hoped that someone would take care of them. I had already emptied my apartment, so I felt stuck. I felt like I didn't have a choice but to go and I cried the entire way. The decision to go cost me a lot and it was just the start of many red flags.

He didn't give me much control of the house. He told me what I could and could not do. I didn't bring a lot because his house was fully furnished. Plus, as I was figuring out what to take he informed that my furniture was junk and that he didn't want it at his house. Truthful, it was secondhand furniture, but it was mine. There was a small room downstairs that he allowed me to put my things in— like pictures, books and my TV. It was my quiet room and I still have a quiet room this day. It's my sanctuary. Mornings are the most important time for me. where I can go to God with it all…good and bad. Sometimes I read. Sometimes I cry. Sometimes and just sit and thank Him for my life. It's so funny that there are days when I wish there was a manual to follow for life, so we never have to go through moments of despair or loss; but it's never too late to change what the future looks like.

The entire year was stressful. I moved out three times, twice staying in a hotel until I found an affordable apartment. It was month to month and after three months he convinced me to move back in. One day, he came home from work and called my room a shrine. He would often complain about me watching Joyce Meyer or T.D. Jakes. After another year of complete misery, I remember sitting in the back of a dark closet, crying out to God for an answer of what to do with my life. I was tired. I was tired of the abuse on both our parts.

I mean I wasn't a saint. Sometimes, I refer to myself as kinda bougie and kinda hood. I wasn't scared of him and would cuss him out just as he would cuss me out. Break up and make up. So many times I tried to pack up and leave, only to have him talk me into staying. The relationship was toxic. We would also fuss and cuss all the way to Church when we went. When we would reconcile we said we would go to church and that would help our relationship.

Once we entered the Church, we pretended to be a happy couple. No sooner than we left Church, we were back at it!

But it was in that closet, I believed that God would speak to me. I was desperate. I remember like it was yesterday. I was watching Bishop TD Jakes and he clearly spoke to anyone watching by TV. I know he was speaking to me. He talked about the lepers who obeyed God when he told them to go wash in the pool. The Bible said they were healed as they went. Bishop said, "I don't know who this is for, but God is telling you to go." He said, "don't worry about what you are leaving behind." The very next day, while my friend was at work, I packed up my car. Whatever didn't fit, I left. I had $200 to my name. I was afraid, but I trusted God. I called my sister and told her I was coming.

There is nothing wrong with change,
if it's in the right direction.
-Winston Churchill

DO IT
AFRAID

I cried most of the way to Charlotte. I was broke and broken. I know I was doing the right thing, but I was still scared. I didn't have a job. But just as I needed a place to stay, my sister needed me to be there. Her husband traveled for work, so she was home with her daughter, and she was pregnant with her second daughter. She has helped me out so many times during my addiction. Even after the many times that I had stolen from her and told lies, she never wavered to help me. She is the person who was there for me, even when I couldn't be there for myself. She has cheered me to my greatest heights. It was my turn to help her. It was a long ride to NC. I had to pull over a number of times because the tears were many. I mean I cried that ugly just about the entire way. I was listening to Yolanda Adams' cd and y'all know her songs will make you cry. My mom and my niece and nephew were heading back to Pittsburg from visiting my sister, so we met at a halfway point. Mom encouraged me we, all hugged and onward I went. Still crying, but I was not looking back.

I got there and unpacked the few items that I had. My sister hooked me up with getting car insurance and a bank account. I knew I needed a job, so after about a week of just repositioning myself I applied for a stylist position at Great Clips. I was called in for an interview and offered a management position, and I accepted. My sister had her second child and it was so much fun hanging out with them. My sister's oldest daughter would always come in my bedroom and watch me get dressed or she would come and say goodnight. There were still bad days for me; my sissy would come home, and I would be crying. I cried because I felt like I should have been further along in my life. I didn't have much money and I here I was the oldest and I was living with her, the baby sister. She would comfort me by saying, "Sissy, it is going to be all right".

After eight months of working on my 400 FICO score and working at Great Clips, I was able to buy my very first house. We called creditors and disputed a lot of items on my credit report and within six months, my score had gone up to over 600. I was so grateful. My sister had come through like she had so many times before. I was finally a homeowner. I was also able to save enough money to furnish my entire house. The day I closed on my house, I slept on the floor with towels and blankets as my bed. I was so excited that I wanted to stay there. Within three months, I had all of the furniture that I needed. I couldn't believe it. But then again, I could, because God is great! There is no one like Him.

God had shown up in time and one time, just as He did the last time. My journey from WV, where my addiction started, to the place I am today. God has been right there. He has been navigating my way, working on my heart and my mind; repositioning me to where he needs me to be. At the time I'm writing this book, I'm still in the same house. I still work at Great Clips in a leadership position— fifteen years later.

Sometimes I still cry, but now they are tears of worship, of gratitude. I have another car now, new furniture and a flat screen TV in every room. God has been good. He still is good. "Won't He do it!" I'm so grateful for my journey; but I wish that I wouldn't have lost so much stuff along the way! I lost a lot - my son's childhood toys and pictures. I feel sad when I hear other parents talk about their children's dolls or action figures that they still have from when their children were young. I still think about how angry and embarrassed he must have felt as a teenager living with his Nana. We got evicted due to my addiction. There were times when he had to sleep on the couch at my mom's house. He was so tall that his feet would hang over the couch's armrest. He never complained but you could see the hurt every day. He has always been a loner, spending much of his free time playing video games or on the computer.

He graduated High School in Las Vegas. He has spent his last two years of High School there with his dad. It was the best thing for him. He was happy there. I went to the graduation, along with my mom and my sister. I was so proud. The two years had done him well.

Our relationship, and his relationship with his other family members was strained. Distance makes the heart grow fonder, right? Well, in this case, the hearts grew apart. The family never reached out to him and he never reached out to anyone. He ended up going into the Air Force. His dad retired from the Air Force, so I think that was something they had spoken about while he was in High school. We didn't talk much while he was in basic training and his first duty station was Germany. He liked Germany and he said all the women there liked him!! (Laughing)

Next, he was stationed in Maryland. There, he met his lady love and eventually got married. They would often come to visit at Christmas time. She was a hoot! We always had a great time when they came home to visit.

His wife ended up pregnant and I was elated! They found out that they were having a girl. Yay! Our family is full of girls. Girls rule, right ladies? I was going to be a Mina. I visited them after she was born and they came to visit in Charlotte, too.

Unfortunately, she passed away at two months old. SIDS. I remember just like it was yesterday. My son called me in the middle of the night and said frantically, "Mom, Leilani died!" I couldn't believe what I was hearing. Crying uncontrollably, he said again, "Leilani is dead!" I was on the road the next day. The family all gathered at their home. We were all completely devastated. Some family was able to stay on base because their apartment was not that big to accommodate everyone. It wasn't the best time, but we had a good time together. We hadn't spent time together in years.

It's normal to question why God would allow such a young baby to die. She was only two months old, but I trust Him. I don't understand it, but I trust it all. Not long after her passing the kids' marriage fell apart— not uncommon. I've heard of so many couples who couldn't get past the death of a child. My son was the last one to check on her. I often wonder if he blamed himself. Guilt is crippling to anyone. Unanswered questions can take a toll on the mind. So can not forgiving. We have to forgive ourselves. It has been my constant prayer that they both forgive themselves and each other.

He left Maryland and was stationed in Colorado. He stopped in Charlotte to spend a few days with me before his long drive. He brought me two totes full of baby clothes, most of them things she never had a chance to wear. I still have them. He just wanted me to hold on to them. And I will until he tells me otherwise.

He didn't expect to be in Colorado long, nor did he want to be there, at first. He wanted to be closer to his family and that was fine with me. I wanted him closer. A few years had come and gone, and he was getting settled in

Colorado, but his heart still wasn't there. He called me about an apartment he was moving into. He said it was expensive, but he liked it. He was excited about buying furniture. We talked a lot after he settled in Colorado. His heart still wanted to be closer to his family, but the opportunity just didn't come.

He ended up meeting and dating a wonderful young woman. I think she was my son's savior in so many ways. She embraced everything that he was and everything that he wasn't. She encouraged him through his sadness. She supported and believed in him. For that, I am so grateful. I was so honored and happy to meet her one year when he came home for Christmas. I would always decorate the house, put up three Christmas trees and have the family over when he came home. It was such a great time. Christmas is my favorite holiday. And I love when he comes home for Christmas!

Not only was she a huge part of my son gradually moving on from his childhood hurts, his failed marriage and loss of his daughter; her family embraced him as well. Ronda was his comfort—his peace. Her family became his family. They accepted him as their own. They exposed him to a life of comfort and togetherness. They were a close family. Just as our family once was; but we lost our closeness years ago and we haven't been able to get it back. Not really sure we have all tried. A few years ago, he confided in me that he was considering changing his last name to Green, her family name. At that moment I knew he still didn't feel a part of our family. Too many years had passed, too many unspoken words, too many missed phone calls.

About a year ago, he decided to go ahead and change his name. My mom was so angry, just like most of our family was when they found out. Everyone had their own idea, their own opinion of why he did it; but no one called and asked him. There was a lot of assuming and fussing; but no one ever reached out to ask him why. So many times we talk about each other, but not to each other. Our family seldom talks to each other. It saddens me. But we definitely talk at each other or about each other. I shared with my son that our actions have consequences—good or bad and he would have to deal with his. I also told him that our choices are not going to please everyone, and we don't have to apologize for our decisions. Now I am not suggesting that he goes around with his middle finger up at family members who are angry with him, but he can hold his head up. I'm not upset over the name change at all. I don't agree with it, but I understand it.

I mean I don't think deciding to join a gang is the answer for replacing a family or forming a family, but I understand why people choose gang life. They want to feel a part of something—a family. Brandon hasn't felt like a part of our family for many years.

The journey for him has been long. Like me, he has had to fight through doubt, anger and depression. It wasn't our family that helped him conquer his demons, it was the Green family. Our family was there for him when he was a child and for that, I'm forever grateful, but no has reached out to him as an adult. Our family wasn't there at the airport when he got back from Afghanistan, she was. No one reached out when he went to Colorado, reluctant and afraid trying to find his way, they were.

He married Ronda—his "light in the darkness." They got married in Mexico. It was my first time out of the country, but rest assure I intend on utilizing my passport. Who would have thought, me, a passport…Mexico. We had a good time. Only mom, Derrick and I went to the wedding. Brandon and I danced to Bruno Mars 24k song.

We rocked it too. That is my jam!!! They are expecting twins and I cannot wait to be a grandma Mina.

I believe God knew why my late granddaughter's clothes were brought to me to keep. A few days ago, I mailed them to Brandon and Ronda.

I tell people all the time that Brandon has had more problems out of me than I have ever had out of him. He was a great kid and has grown into an awesome young man. Our relationship is constantly being restored. He shares with me. Even small things like cutting his own hair, or when he buys some new gadget. He also asked me on a number of occasions if I would consider moving to Colorado, a great sign that he loves me and wants me around; and for that I'm grateful.

Your life does not get better
by chance. It gets better by change.
-Jim Rohn

SET YOUR MIND
AND KEEP IT SET

I soon started to date. I felt lonely and I wanted to fill the void, so I allowed myself to date men who were not available. I don't mean physically, most men will make themselves available for sex, but I'm speaking in terms of mentally and emotionally. Women tend to go after what looks good and feels good, rather than what *is* good. I had a house and a car, and I worked, so I had something to offer. I'm attractive with a good vibe. I'm smart. But parts of me were still broken. But, we as women sometimes allow men to treat us any kind of way, just to say that we have a man. I remember this one guy I met at a club. He was cute. As I was leaving, he was just getting out of his truck. It was a nice truck, so I assumed he worked. Looks are deceiving though, right? We spoke, and he went in the club. I decided to leave a note on his truck to call me. He actually called the next day. We went out a couple of times and I finally invited him over. I should have taken heed of the red flags…phone constantly ringing and him going outside to talk. Women should trust our gut. We know. We just choose to ignore the signs.

After a couple of weeks of not showing up when he said he was coming over or not calling when he said he would call, I mustered up enough self-esteem to say to myself and mean it "you are worthy and wonderful". I never called him again. We would see each other in the club, and I would speak to him. I wasn't angry with him. He was who he was; however, I made it clear who I was. I was at peace with not having a man. I actually spent the next year celibate, just living life. I worked and hung out with my sister friend, just doing girl stuff like shopping and going to have a glass of wine by the lake.

But I prayed for a good man, tall, dark and handsome, no small kids and one that would love only me. I accepted that, for now, it was my time to spend with God. My time to enjoy Him. I realized that it was an opportunity of not having the responsibility of a relationship. Relationships are work. My time with God became so important. I enjoyed it. I would get up in the morning and read, listen to meditation music on television, (DAYSTAR REFLECTIONS is my favorite) other times I would pray. There were many times that I would walk around my house from room to room and I would just be in worship mode because God had (has) been so good. I would think of how far I'd come from the crack house to owning a house and I would just cry uncontrollably. I was so grateful. So humbled. I couldn't believe that I actually owned a house, but then again I could believe it.

God is good. So good. Still good. There were still bouts of fear, doubt, low self-esteem, but I yearned for the ability to take the growth steps that will mean a totally better life. And I have come to learn that all of us can take steps—no matter how small— in the direction we want to go. Taking small steps leads the way to taking larger steps later on. I believe that each time I took a step some measure of increased faith and self-esteem was unto me.

This one particular night my sister friend called and wanted to go out. I said no, at first. I was tired, I had worked all day and I was also tired of going out. She talked me into it. We both agreed that we'd go out for a couple hours and we would leave. One of the guys that I had dated briefly was there and introduced us to his friend. My friend's aim was to hook up with me and have his friend hook up with my girl. Uh, not. His friend was tall and fine! He had a deep voice and his demeanor was very laid back. I thought, hmmmm.

We ordered drinks, sat at the table and laughed about what people had on in the club. After an hour or so, my girl and I left. Through a few minutes of small lies I got the number from my guy friend to call his friend from the club. I told him it was for my sister friend, but actually I wanted to speak with him. I called him and we ended up talking for hours. That voice of his, though!! We went on a date and for drinks and dinner. We continued to see each a couple times a week. We both worked different shifts, and a month later went on our first beach trip together.

We made arrangements to introduce each other to our families and it wasn't long after many dates and time spent together that we both committed to just dating each other. Five years later we are still a couple. It's a funny thing I used to schedule my days off around his days off. You know how it is when you first start dating you wanted to spend every waking hour together. But after a couple of years together I now make sure our days off are not together. Girl I need my space (laughing) and he enjoys his down time as well. We are also puppy parents and having days off opposite of each other helps us curve our doggy daycare spending.

I believe it was truly divine intervention. Derrick has all the qualities that I prayed for. When I finally shared with him about my past, he wasn't sure he wanted to date, nor commit to someone like me. Even though my life was totally different, he had reservations. But after watching my lifestyle, the consistency of my desire to do better, be better and have better his feeling of uncertainty subsided. I'm not sure what he thinks of me putting my story out to the world because he hasn't said how he feels about it. But, as I mentioned in the early chapter of this book, my story has to be told. Someone needs my story. We have been together now for 6 years and it has been good. There have been times of readjusting and reestablishing our relationship because we both have changed as we grow. Even in relationships we are all a work in progress. I can say, without a shadow of a doubt, that this is the healthiest relationship I have been in, in over 30 years.

LIVING
WITHOUT REGRET

To Thine Own Self Be True. I'm not sure where I read that, but I like it. As children, we are taught what not to say and what not to do. We are taught to do as we are told. In a crazy way, we are taught other people matter and we don't! We were taught not to tell the truth about what we really feel, what we think or what we want. There were lines in my family like "do what I say, not what I do." But really, I did what I saw my mom do. She was promiscuous with men, so was I. She lied, so did I. She sold and used drugs, so did I. Not only did you have to listen to your parents and elders, but eventually employers and other people in authority. You learned that telling the truth about adults' wrongdoings and being hypocrites was not talked about! Like the times when mother would tell us to tell the bill collector that she was not home when they called, when in fact she was. But when we lied about where we were when she asked and found out differently, we got a beaten.

Unlike when I was a child I now realize that I matter. I'm not afraid anymore—I'm not afraid to tell the truth, even if the person gets mad. I've learned to speak in love. I've learned to honor myself by saying "no" if that's what I wanted to say. I've learned to honor myself by saying that I don't want to go somewhere or do something. I've learned how to stay home and take care of me. It's very empowering. It's very rewarding. Becoming aware of yourself is not easy. You have to accept yourself without judgement. Every detail of your life has to be revisited... often.

I cannot say I am a religious person. At least, not in the sense that I do not attend church. I also cuss a little and drink wine. But, my faith is very important to me. I really do strive to make my words and what I share on social media match how I live. When I share posts they are usually motivational quotes or positive affirmations because I believe it can make an impact in people's lives. My life is no accident. Everything was purposed for this season and my job as I see it is to give something of myself that will help others. If I had to describe my life's work it would be honoring the life in me through my everyday choices to help another woman along the way.

Change is hard at first, messy in the middle,
and gorgeous at the end.
-Robin Sharma

BUT GOD

I recently celebrated 20 years as a manager with Great Clips. It's an achievement to say the least and I couldn't be more proud to be a part of such a great company. Great Clips is the number one haircare brand in the country. Woohoo!! I also run one of the top salons in the Charlotte NC market. Yup me!! I have a great team. We have broken a couple of records in the past couple of years and I pray that we can hit an historical record by the end of this year. It would be perfect because I have decided in addition to writing this book I am going to start a new journey in Health and Life Coaching. I believe there is more to unfold for me. I have been thinking about it for a while but that voice that always tells you that you can't, or it will never work because you're too old, you know the voice. I really haven't been happy with cutting hair for years. I love being in a leadership position...developing teams... but not happy cutting hair anymore. I'm at a place where I don't want to be held back by not making a change. Another change.

One thing I realize is that in life change is constant and most of the time it's necessary. Coaching is a calling. Thank you, LIFE, for getting me to this place of awesomeness and alignment.

IN CONCLUSION

Because of what happened to me, I'm stronger, I'm wiser. I make better decisions. The longer you are in faith the easier it becomes to see how all along God has kept me. When you experience Him, you trust Him. Every change has come because of Him. Sharing my story is both heartbreaking and inspiring and in a lot of ways this is where real spiritual transformation is occurring. God is here. He is real. He looks lovingly down from heaven and sees me. He sees you.

I hope this book has inspired you to give your life a long hard look and discover things that you may need to change. Girl look, I know first-hand how hard and unappealing it may be to start self-examining yourself. But know that there is also hope to get from where you are to where you want to be. Don't lose your hope. The world needs your story. It needs your courage. God wants the best for us, but there is one thing that can stop us from experiencing His best, and that's US!!

There is no such thing as perfect, only evolving or as my beautiful former 1st lady Michelle Obama titled her book "Becoming". I mean for a while we can have it our way, doing what we want, buying all the new technology gadgets, new clothes and cars. Those things give temporary relief of what we really desire, and that is knowing God. If you think you are in a better position without Him, have at it.

…But If nothing changes, nothing changes.

ABOUT THE AUTHOR

Missy draws on her own life experiences of addiction, family disfunction and abuse to bring women all over the world a message of courage, hope, healing and change. She enjoys quiet evenings in her backyard, and she loves to travel anywhere that has sandy beaches.

CPSIA information can be obtained
at www.ICGtesting.com
Printed in the USA
LVHW041304061020
668071LV00016B/887